D0818271

STUDENT
STUDY
SKILLS

A
How to Learn
Guide

Will Clark

STUDENT STUDY SKILLS

Copyright © 2010 by Will Clark

ISBN 1452863660

All rights reserved. No part of this book may be reproduced or copied in any form or by any means, electronic or mechanical, including photocopying or recording, or by any information storage and retrieval system, without permission, in writing, from the author.

Published By
Motivation Basics
P.O. Box 6327
Diamondhead, MS 39525
228-255-5019
Will01@aol.com

For more information visit the author at:
AuthorsDen.com

CONTENTS

GOALS OF THIS BOOK

To help students learn how to learn by understanding the process and by accepting the idea that they have gifted abilities and success potential and are capable of wonderful achievements. Those wonderful achievements, however, must be earned with sincere effort and dedication to the task of learning. Society owes them nothing but opportunity to develop their success potential. Each student chooses his or her own success or failure; that choice often made from home, peer, or other cultural or natural influences and conditions.

To encourage parents who don't know how to help their children learn to accept that important and necessary task. It's the most important part of the education process, and cannot and should not be left as merely a teacher and education establishment task. Most teachers are dedicated to their profession, but they cannot learn for a student and should not be the focus of parents' and students' failures.

4

A Basic Learning Experience

The other end of my cotton row was a long way off. Most times I couldn't even see that end because the rows curved in several places. In the Central Mississippi hill country cultivated rows were curved around the slope's contour to keep dirt from washing away during hard rains. Cotton rows followed the same curves as the heavy-duty terraces placed at certain intervals, their closeness depending on the severity of the slope. I had been down these rows many times already and, although I couldn't see the end, I knew how far it was. It was a long way, and looked forever away for a bare-foot, ten-year-old boy.

I had seen cotton rows in the flat lands of the Mississippi Delta. They were straight, but so long one couldn't see the end of those either; some as long as a mile. I wondered how one could ever get to the other end of those.

Early in the growing season rain was welcome to make the cotton seed explode, but while that happened grass and weeds usually drank first and surged well ahead of the cotton plants, selfishly trying to leave none for their later rival. At that time, in the early nineteen-fifties, herbicides were not available, especially for small-acre farmers. The only dependable herbicide was a hoe, a tool with a handle much longer than the height of most ten-year-olds. Some still exist today, most in historical museums or propped in a seldom visited corner of a hardware store. In the nineteen-fifties, and before, it was the weapon of choice to fight grass and weeds in cotton and corn fields. Special pride blossomed from those who owned one with the best shape or the sharpest edge. When I was the youngest in the

5

field, mine was always the most dulled reject with which I had to beat grass and weeds into submission rather than cut them with a sharp edge.

Chopping cotton was long, hard, and tedious work for a ten-year-old or one of any age. Just getting to the other end of one row was challenging. That process, seemingly simple, was more complex than could be imagined by one lacking that experience. The process could even be compared to saving a new-born baby from dangerous bullies. That new, fragile plant, only three or four inches tall, often was strangled by tenacious and hard grass and weeds. Why, then, the complicated process? Hoeing (chopping) the grass too close to the cotton plant often destroyed the fragile plant. Not hoeing close enough or deep enough left determined grass continuing its death stranglehold. It was difficult not to destroy the plant when the dirt was either too hard or too soft and flaky. Too many destroyed plants left the cotton field too sparse for a profitable yield. Too much grass created the same result, with stunted cotton plants. Sixty years later I still remember that process: leave three or four plants standing in a group, each group a little more than the width of a hoe blade apart. That allowed the removal of grass from all four sides of the plant, not just two sides.

For a profitable yield, serious decisions were required with every stroke of that hoe. Even with a perfect yield, our three-acre cotton farm was unprofitable. Only three acres were authorized for my family under the acreage allotment system at that time. My friends think I'm joking when I say I was raised on a three-acre cotton patch. Although only three acres, there was always hope for a higher acreage allotment and a better yield next year. Those anticipated better years never came for small hill farmers.

My responsibility expanded when I was fourteen. Until then my great-uncle plowed the field with a hand-held plow pulled by a horse or mule. He was a share-cropper for a larger farmer, and plowed our field during his spare time. His father, my great-grandfather, had also been a share-cropper after the end of the Civil War. At fourteen,

I assumed that duty. I was surprised to learn the basic task was the same as hoeing, but the responsibilities were greater. For example, the horse or mule was a living creature who required care, concern, and nourishment. The extent of that concern was often determined by the type of plow the animal had to pull, the time of day, and the time of year.

Basic preparation of the soil was performed with a plow called a middle-buster. It was a deep running plow which threw dirt from both sides to form half a new row on both sides. A pass in the center of the next old row formed the new planting row in what had been the trail the previous planting season. A turning plow had a blade on one side forming half a middle-buster which finished forming the planting row and added more dirt volume. The sweep plow was a skimming blade angled out on both sides to cut and remove weeds and grass in the trails between the raised planted rows. A side-harrow was a springy rake-like device that loosened the soil when it became too tightly compacted near the plants.

The horse or mule required more rest when pulling the deeper running plows. They also needed more water and rest during the summer months. It wasn't uncommon for horses or mules to suffer heatstroke, and even die, if they were not cared for responsibly. While following behind that horse or mule, I always knew the animal needed more rest and water than I did. I never allowed my plow animal to be jeopardized.

Just as close attention was necessary not to destroy cotton plants when hoeing, more attention was necessary when plowing. Little things became crucial and didn't permit the luxury of a wandering mind. Running the plow too shallow created an uneven and ineffective planting bed. Running it too deep was arduous for the animal. Depth was controlled by tilting the handles. Allowing the sweep plow to wander often destroyed plants on either side. A thoughtless nudge on one of the long reins would suggest the plow animal wander into the planted row. Inattention to the plow blade often resulted in jolting to a sudden stop when hitting a stump, or stepping with bare feet onto a bed of unearthed, newly-hatched snakes. I was jolted by many hidden stumps. Fortunately, the twisting movements of a snake bed always allowed me time to jump from that danger, since the snakes were probably more startled than I, and I was quite nimble at that young age.

Those long rows weren't any shorter while following a plow. They were still from 'one end to the other.' Even when the crop was 'laid by' those rows were as long as ever, their length still seeming endless. The term 'laid by' indicated the end to hoeing and plowing, and the crop left to finish maturing, usually about mid summer, depending upon the rain. At this time we scattered dry field peas in the laid by corn field, hoping for a bountiful side crop of field peas. Thus the name 'field peas.'

Even after the field was laid by, cotton was a special case requiring constant work, and more walks down those long rows to wage war on boll weevils. They were relentless, and destroyed the hopes, dreams, and finances of many small-acreage farmers who couldn't afford more effective equipment or more insecticide to win the battle. Vaguely, I recall an arsenic-based insecticide that was very effective but was quickly removed from the market since it was determined to be a health and environmental hazard. That was after I walked those long rows many times blowing that insecticide dust from a hand-cranked blower strapped to my chest. The apparatus had two trailing ducts that blew the dusty insecticide at the cotton boll level. Certainly, I absorbed more insecticide than did the intended targets. It was so effective that common houseflies disappeared from around our house and barn for two weeks.

Picking cotton was no less arduous, but the concept of long rows was different. If the cotton yield was sparse, the other end arrived too quickly because there wasn't enough mature cotton to pick. Either rain, boll weevils, or fertilizer quality had spoiled the yield. Picking cotton in the same row for a long time was the most desirable.

Seemingly simple, picking cotton also had many potential

hazards that required close attention and care. An open cotton boll became hard with spiny points when it opened to let the cotton fibre dry in the hot summer sun. Only those most experienced could pick cotton without pricking their fingers with those sharp points. Often those pricks would result in serious infections. Snakes also cooled themselves under the shade of dense cotton plants. It wasn't unusual to see one slither away when a cool area was approached. Ordinarily, moccasins and rattlesnakes would leave early, but the copperhead was always more aggressive and reluctant to give up an area. It was more practical, however, to run instead of trying to determine the snake's species. Wasp nests were another unwelcome surprise while focusing on pulling cotton from a beautiful hand-sized, prickly cotton boll.

The horses patiently waited while the vacuum tube at the cotton gin sucked the twelve hundred pounds of cotton from the wagon. That volume usually produced a cotton bale of about eight hundred pounds, the remaining four hundred pounds being cotton seed that could be sold to the gin for resale, or returned to the wagon to save for planting the next year. Value of the bale was determined after a grader examined the quality and length of the fibre. Our farm usually produced two bales, the total value of which never recovered the costs of raising the crop. That was even considering that my time in the effort was zero value, for a period of four years.

In the summer between my sophomore and junior years of high school I finally found a real job working for someone else. I delivered groceries on a bicycle for a small grocery store in New Orleans. I don't remember the name of the store, but it was on the corner of Sycamore Street and South Carrollton Avenue.

Those months, June through August, were hot and oppressive twelve hours a day, six days a week, but that eighteen dollars a week was real money I could spend. In that job, there were only four major hazards to avoid. One was to get to my destination without spilling the groceries in the basket on front of my bike. When I did, I always had eggs in the basket. Second was to avoid the child welfare inspector. Third was not to spend all my money at the Frostop Root

Beer stores trying to stay cool. Fourth was to avoid the girl, my age, who lived two houses south of the store. She indicated she wanted to be friendly, but that was something totally outside my realm of experience. I knew about cotton, not girls. When I knew she was waiting for my return, I always took the long way back to the store. I survived that summer and returned home with about thirty dollars.

During the summer between my junior and senior years, I worked for my uncle Frank in Hortense, Georgia cutting and hauling pulpwood. Although the motions were different, the process was similar to farming cotton. In cotton, the process was one row at a time. In pulpwood, it was one pine tree at a time. Looking at all the rows, or all the trees, made the task seem difficult, if not impossible. Accepting the task of processing only one row or one tree, although not pleasant at the time, allowed the concept of reasonable success to be instilled.

As with cotton farming there were many hazards to avoid, and hazards in the forest had more dangerous consequences. Our equipment consisted of three chain saws and two small pulpwood trucks.

At seventeen, I was the oldest of the three boys operating the chain saws. Although careful, I still have a large scar on my left elbow where a chain saw blade hit it from only a minor distracted moment. Fortunately for me, it tore off only a strip of skin, without any muscle or bone damage. Although becoming proficient in felling a pine tree in the intended direction, occasionally one would twist with the falling motion and move in another direction. Worse yet was the tree that wouldn't fall and instead would kick from the bottom with a sudden release.

Once the tree was felled it was trimmed then cut into four-foot segments. Even the simple process of trimming the felled tree held many hidden hazards that required total focus. Sometimes the chain saw would bounce from a springy limb. Neither was it uncommon for a half-trimmed limb to release and allow the tree to fall on an out-of-place foot.

Once the trees were trimmed and cut, the five-foot pieces were loaded by hand onto the truck into a volume called a cord. If I remember correctly a cord of pulpwood was five feet high, five feet wide, and ten feet long. The truck bed was about three feet off the ground, which meant the top layer of wood was about eight feet high. The higher the layer rose, the more dangerous it became to load, by hand. Many times did I jump away to avoid a two-hundred pound piece of wood from sliding awry at the top and falling on my head. Even that simple act of stacking a cord of pulpwood required planning and care, since all the pieces were not straight and level. Those little logs had to fit together like a puzzle to be safe and stable. Inattention was an invitation to certain disaster. Even today, with all the mechanization available for workers, the forest is still a dangerous work environment.

I earned a dollar for each cord we processed. That totaled about eighteen dollars each week; three cords a day, six days a week. The fifty dollars in my pocket when I returned home to start school that fall was enough to buy a bolt-action Remington shotgun for squirrel hunting that winter. I shot one squirrel, watched it look at me as it died in agony, and never shot another. I sold that shotgun for thirty-six dollars after I graduated from high school, in 1957, to have money when I left home to join the Air Force.

Understanding goals, hazards, determination, and results from focused efforts has guided my success and happiness. I learned these common concepts apply to all positive life efforts, and it's with this background and experience that I offer them to help improve educational aspirations for those with the willingness, insight, and courage to try.

Perhaps those without gifted backgrounds or ability who refuse to allow small, natural, and positive steps guide them to the end of the row will never get there. They look at the forest, not at the tree. They look at the cotton field, not the row. They only wish for success instead of seeing, accepting, and taking those little steps necessary to lead them there. Their other option is despair and failure.

11

Personal success, including education, is a personal choice. No one, or no society, can choose it for or force it upon another person.

Unfortunately, many choose despair and failure when they refuse to accept the positive options given to us by our Creator and our country, fought for by those who sacrificed everything to form our nation, and defended by those who, still today, give their lives in service to permit those personal choices. Success is by doing; not by hoping.

TEN

PARENTING HELP SKILLS

Some parents who complain most about the poor quality of teachers and the lack of motivation and understanding of students are, themselves, weak in the education process. There probably are some weak and incompetent teachers. There probably are some teachers who are otherwise competent, but who have such personalities that students are afraid to go near their classrooms. Also, many students aren't naturally motivated to use good student skills. They need more encouragement and direction.

These areas in the education system must be considered to help make the education system work effectively. However, these weaknesses cannot be determined until parents have fulfilled their important roles in their children's education. Parents must continue to be involved in the total education process. First, however, they must insure their actions, or lack of actions, give their children a positive attitude to learn rather than a negative attitude toward learning. Parents provide the first level and the first influence to their children's learning. They are the roots to learning. Ordinarily, the teacher's influence is only secondary.

Following are ten teaching skills for parents to help their children learn. Unless the child is naturally gifted, the parent must use these skills to help prepare a child a teacher can teach.

13

1

Be a Learning Partner

A child should not face the learning process alone. Parents too often fail to help their children learn, for they merely assume the teaching and learning process is a task shared between the school and the child. Perhaps some parents really believe this; others may use this belief as a convenient excuse not to get involved. Furthermore, some parents feel inadequate to help their children with homework and other studies.

Regardless of the reason or the excuse, that reason or that excuse isn't big enough for parents to avoid the responsibility to help their children learn. The parent must be the child's learning partner, regardless of the parent's ability, intelligence, or education level. The parent must participate to provide the child with the confidence, the comfort, the aspirations, the approval, and the safety the child must have to focus on learning. Otherwise, the child will be distracted from learning by focusing on those other missing essentials.

The excuse that many parents use for not helping their children learn is that they, "Just don't have time." A one parent family often uses that one parent status as a rational justification. Two parent families use the same excuse, "It takes both of us to make a good living, and we just don't have time." Ordinarily, these people who complain most that they don't have time to help their children learn are the same people who complain most about the quality of teachers and schools. It's easier to place the blame on someone else.

Many parents, persuaded by political and social rhetoric, are more strongly supporting the belief that education is the responsibility of schools and teachers. This idea that school systems and teachers are responsible for a child's education is a narrow view of education. Parents must understand the broad view of education to make the learning process work. Education consists of three parts, not just one part or one view, as is generally accepted by those who try to avoid responsibility.

Teaching is only one part of the education process. Schools are responsible for providing facilities and teachers to provide instruction. Schools and teachers are also responsible for creating conditions that will allow student motivation. They are not most responsible for direct student motivation. They are responsible for teaching.

Learning is another part of the education process. Schools and teachers are not responsible for student learning. That process must be accomplished by a student. This student activity, or student involvement, is called 'studying.' A teacher or a school cannot do this function for a student. Studying has no short cuts, nor any quick answers. It must be done, methodically, and by each student, personally and individually.

However, a basic concept of this book is that schools and teachers don't teach students this learning process. The education system, as well as our frustrated society, seems more willing to accept the popular idea that our education problem lies in the lack of quality in our teachers. The acceptable conclusion is that if we have better teachers, we will have better education. Our education system is more focused on teaching than on learning. Since each student must learn - and not teach - learning must be our target to improve education effectiveness. The quality of learning is more important than the quality of teaching. The purpose for this book is to improve that learning quality. Parents are a vital part of that learning process.

Motivation is the third part of learning. The motivation to learn must come from within the child. Neither the parent nor the teacher can 'motivate' a child, or anyone else. A person must be motivated from within. Screaming at a child, offering money and concessions to a child, and giving a motivational speech to a child do not motivate a child. These things might give information to a child to help him or her decide to fulfill a need. Nevertheless, that decision comes from within based upon that child's needs - at that point in time. Most likely, the motivating needs for a child who must endure a critical or condescending motivational lecture from a parent would be simply to escape from that uncomfortable situation.

Parents share in the responsibility to help their children find ways to fulfill their important needs. Through nurturing, loving guidance, and example, a parent must lead the child to feel the needs that are important. Once these needs are felt by a child, the child will create his or her own self motivation to become successful. In this case, successful in making an effort to study and learn.

Parents bring their own children into this world, therefore they are responsible for guiding the development of their children. Schools and teachers are only part of that development. They are not responsible for that development. Parents must be learning partners with their children to guide them through the frustrations, hardships, and difficulties of the learning process.

17

2

Focus on Effort - Not Grades

Good grades must be considered rewards, not goals. Parents, as well as the education system generally, are narrowly focused on students' grades rather than the process and goals that must be reached to receive good grades. Effort and work are the actions. Grades are the results of those actions. A student cannot make grades. A student can take actions, knowledgeable study, that may produce good grades. An athletic event may be used as an example of this concept.

In a typical athletic event, such as a hundred-yard dash, the runner wants to do his or her best. That person wants to be prepared at the time of the race to do his or her best. To be prepared, that person must be at his or her maximum physical and mental capability at the moment of the race. While preparing to be physically and mentally ready, that person cannot concentrate on the trophy as being the goal. That person must focus on being physically and mentally prepared to get to the finish line in the quickest possible time. This preparation must be the goal. If the runner has at least equal ability as other runners and has prepared better, that person will win the race. The trophy for winning will be the reward - not the goal.

Parents, even those with knowledge and good intentions, often focus on the wrong goals when trying to motivate their children to learn. They emphasize grades and not the effort to earn those grades. One question emphasizes this concept: How many parents offer money to their children for grades, instead of time and effort to produce those grades?

3

Keep Communications Open

The basic purpose for a parent is to provide care, training, and guidance for a child. The requirements for physical care are easy to fulfill. A parent understands those physical needs, for we all have the same basic physical needs. Fulfilling emotional and psychological needs requires other considerations.

A child's emotional needs are determined by more subtle factors often hidden by unseen doubts and fears. Each person has his or her individual emotional needs based on his or her life experiences and perceptions. It's unlikely all those experiences and perceptions

Reading Opens Learning Doors

will be exposed to parents. Often the child does not recognize his or her own emotional needs. These experiences and perceptions must be viewed and understood through open and sincere communications between the parent and child.

Open and sincere communications never develop in some families that allow parents to have a guiding influence over the child's development. Sometimes the parent causes this lack of development; sometimes the child causes the void. In either case the parent is still responsible for bridging the gap to effective communications. In this case, effective communications aren't specified as those that clearly explain but targeted at those the child can understand and relate to his or her perspectives and needs. To reach this relationship the parent must avoid certain barriers to that communication. Some barriers occur naturally, and some barriers are created by parents as they try to influence their children.

One of those barriers is created by the typical admonition, "Why don't you listen to reason; why don't you understand something this simple?" This is a typical comment some parents make in their frustration to 'get through' to their children. The child ordinarily understands the logic being explained, but that logic doesn't fit the child's needs at that time.

Parents create another typical communications barrier when they criticize their children's undesirable friends. Children have the same feelings about friends as adults. They must defend their friends. This is a built-in emotion that cannot be destroyed by logic. In this case, parents must try to fulfill another emotional need of their children to make the attraction to undesirable friends less forceful.

Many children live in homes that don't encourage, or even allow, them to learn open and sincere communications. Some parents are too selfish to consider the emotional needs of their children. They must dominate all the family activity to satisfy their own ego and esteem needs. Some parents don't understand the value of courtesy upon their children's emotional needs. They don't hesitate to scream

21

at their children to, "Shut up!" and then complain to their children that they don't understand. Other parents simply tell their children they are too young to understand. These are only examples of typical barriers that close communications between parents and children. Parents must use meaningful communications, not personal frustrations, to learn what their children's immediate needs are. Those needs must be recognized to allow real and open communications. Children's basic needs are the same as adults' basic needs. These include a feeling of belonging and comfort, the desire for respect and love, and the right to feel important. These needs begin when a child understands the concept of the word "I."

4

Schedule Talk Time

Communications must not only be open and sincere, communications must also exist for the parent to have any guiding influence over a child. Too often parents and children are too busy to talk to each other. The lack of communicating creates a habit of not communicating. A habit, once created, is hard to overcome. The time that would ordinarily be taken for talking to each other becomes filled with other essential activity that continues to crowd out time that would otherwise be available for talking.

The habit of not taking time to talk with each other must be broken as any other habit is broken. It takes a concerted effort.

Although the concerted effort might seem artificial in the beginning, it must be done. In this case, the habit of not taking time to talk must be replaced by a habit that's more productive. The more productive habit is a scheduled time to talk. Adhering to a schedule, a regularly scheduled time to talk, will force that habit to become as automatic as the habit of not talking.

Each family has its own schedule of times and events. These times and events are determined by ages of family members, location of the home, and family interest in the community. A family with several children who are involved in sports and other activities might have a more difficult challenge finding time for quality conversation than would a family with only one child who's only interested in grades.

Nevertheless, parents must insure quality conversation time exists between themselves and their children. Children must be allowed to learn that good communication skills are important, and parents must allow their children the time and opportunity to express their intelligence, interests, and knowledge. This open expression helps the child develop and reinforce esteem and self-confidence necessary for continuing success.

5

Understand the Learning Process

For most students, grades are determined by the amount and quality of study. Of course, some students are more intelligent than others and make good grades with only little effort. For the average student, however, increased study can offset the small difference in basic intelligence. It's estimated grades are determined approximately sixty percent by intelligence, thirty percent by effort, and ten percent by factors such as random chance.

This conclusion suggests that a student with higher intelligence requires less study time than a student with average intelligence. This conclusion also suggests that a student with only average intelligence can make the same good grades with increased study effort. A student with below average intelligence must make even more effort to make good grades. In either case, study time that reflects that effort must be emphasized more than grades that result from that effort. Frustrated parents often emphasize grades to their children, rather than effort to earn grades. Those parents typically admonish their children to study harder to make good grades. To study harder suggests or implies the student must somehow find a more focused study method or a more intelligent study method for deeper understanding. This concept gives the impression that the child must become more intelligent to study. This typical admonition to a child creates frustration and despair for that child, for only the same level of intelligence exists. The child can't develop more of it in himself or herself. Within a limited time, intelligence can't be increased. Under this handicap of frustration and despair a student loses confidence and esteem.

A parent must emphasize increased study time and study skills to a student who needs to improve his or her grades. A student can understand the concept of studying more or learning study skills, but a student - or anyone else - can't understand the concept of studying harder to make better grades. Better grades should be the result of more study time and better study effort by using effective study skills.

6

Know the Teacher

Parents of successful students ordinarily know their children's teachers. Parents of lower achieving students ordinarily don't know their children's teachers. Is there a cause and effect to these relationships? If so, in which direction? Do parents of successful students learn to know their teachers, or, do students become successful because their parents know their teachers well?

Perhaps these relationships are created both ways. Parents of successful students tend to support their children, and want to be recognized for that support. Consequently, they work with teachers to show their level of concern and support for their children. In turn, teachers ordinarily express their appreciation and respect for that parental support. On the other hand, when parents of less successful students work closely with a teacher, that bonding is ordinarily interpreted by students as sincere concern. That concern becomes adopted by the student who recognizes it.

7

Become Involved

Parents who want their children to become concerned and involved with school and education success must demonstrate that concern themselves. Too often, parents use the excuse that they don't have time to be involved in school activities. Too often, also, these are the same parents with failing or low-achieving students.

Although most parents now work at regular jobs, which is the normal reason for not having time to attend school functions, there are functions and activities that may be attended at times parents aren't working. For example, many parent and teacher organizations and associations ordinarily meet in the evenings, not during the normal workday.

Parents must also make time to fulfill their responsibility to their children. That responsibility is to show by example that school is important; and, that to get the most from school the student must also be involved. Parents must show how that involvement affects concern and attitudes. Simply explaining that involvement is important to their children is not enough. A child is more impressed by what happens, not what is said.

8

Teach Positive Self-Esteem

Children are highly impressionable and hear more than some parents imagine. Children's ears are fine-tuned to the extraordinary, and especially to comments about themselves. For example, a parent might be trying to explain a lesson to a young child, and in frustration might exclaim, "This is so simple anybody should understand it." Even a very young child might interpret this unplanned comment as an indication that he or she is less intelligent than most people. The loss of self-esteem and confidence from this interpretation might cause that child to perform at the level that he or she expects; in that lower status.

What should a parent do when facing a tutoring problem that evokes an unplanned destructive statement while trying to do something positive, helping the child? Before trying to help their children with a school problem or homework parents must plan for these frustrations. They will occur.

Children learn many new ideas and concepts. If they already knew them they wouldn't have to learn them. Learning is not always easy. Therefore, the parent shouldn't expect to be successful each time he or she begins a tutoring session. Sometimes it's better to leave the problem for awhile, or get another person with a different perspective to help. Instead of suggesting the child isn't trying to learn or doesn't want to understand, the parent should transfer the child's attention to something easier to learn to help rebuild that lost confidence.

To help avoid frustration, parents must also know that different children learn in different ways. Some children learn through the sense of hearing - by sound. Some learn by sight - by visualization. Still others learn by feel - by touching. Some children are more adept with numbers than with words. Some can learn music with little effort, and some can never learn the concepts of music. Each child is similar, but unique. Each child has an individual and unique quality, and concept of learning. Trying to use the teaching approach that causes frustration often degrades the child's self esteem, which in turn makes learning more difficult.

During the tutoring process, a parent must be prepared for frustration and not let that frustration cause comments that would harm the child's self-esteem and confidence. The parent must also be prepared to teach with the learning approach that best fits the child's

30

learning, whether it's by sound, touch, or sight.

9

Give Books as Gifts

Gifts are important. Gifts from one person to another reflect a transfer of something valuable or meaningful between people. If the person who gives the gift treats that gift as something of value, so will the recipient of that gift. Books, however, are often given without the transfer of a feeling of value. Therefore, they aren't treated as valuable.

When a parent or other relative gives a book to a child for a special occasion, such as a birthday, the book is usually given as a compromise gift, not as a valuable gift. It's not unusual for the person who gives a book to say, "I was going to get you something special, but I found this book I thought you might like." This statement, or similar statements, are interpreted by the average child as meaning, "I thought about getting you something good, but I decided to get you something not good." In this case the book has no value.

Books should be treated as special gifts - for they are special. Books allow a child's mind to play with the thoughts and feelings of other characters. Toys only allow a child's hands, eyes and imagination to play. And, the child's imagination is limited to the concept of the toy.

Special care must be taken to give value when books are given as gifts, especially to young children. The person who gives a book must give that value by expressing that the book was bought as the perfect gift, not as a compromise gift. The giver of the book must also draw the child into the book by telling the child who the main characters are and what they are trying to do. If the child is not introduced to the characters, he or she might never want to learn more about them.

10

Introduce the Child to the Library

A library is a special place. It's a place where anyone may travel the world, sail all the seas and visit with kings and queens. In a library, a person may participate in a religious feast with a lost native tribe. A person may explore secret caverns and dungeons. And, a person may even rule the world for a few hours. A person may do all these things and many more simply by picking up a different book. And, books are free in a library. A library is the world's best travel bargain.

A library proclaims learning, books, and words are important. A library is the place that records history, heritage, and beliefs. A library is the foundation that represents who we are. Libraries are so important that in ancient times they were the first buildings to be destroyed when one city state or one country conquered another.

TWENTY

STUDENT STUDY SKILLS

Once a student is ready to study and understands the reason for studying, he or she must then get set to study. Getting set requires specific skills and tasks. These skills concern preparing the physical environment for effective study. They and other important study skills will be identified next.

1

Choose a good study area

The first step to create effective study habits is to choose a good study area. Choices in the average home are usually limited to the living room, the kitchen table, a bedroom, or possibly a den.

The location should be a quiet area, such as a bedroom, a den, or study. Trying to create a quiet study area in a routinely noisy area, such as at a kitchen table, is less desirable. In a routinely noisy area, the noise will be anticipated even though it might not be present. Distractions, real or anticipated, are usually magnified for an overly curious child.

The study area should not be so quiet and distant that the child feels isolated or cut off from other people. Although the study area should be relatively quiet, the child should be in an area where he or she may avoid a feeling of isolation.

Lighting conditions are important in the study location. Generally, indirect lighting is less tiring for reading, assuming the light is bright enough. Enough light, in proper locations, should be provided to prevent glare and shadows on or near the reading material. More than one light might be necessary. A child with tired eyes certainly can't concentrate enough to focus totally on the subject.

Adequate ventilation is also necessary in the study area to allow a student to remain alert. The volume of oxygen is reduced in a closed or unventilated area. A student will not be as alert if the oxygen flow is reduced. This often creates drowsiness and lack of full concentration, which may cause ineffective and wasted study efforts.

2

Prepare the study area

When a student goes to the study area to study, he or she

should be prepared to use that time to study. That time shouldn't be wasted searching for materials to help in the study process. Many students use much of their planned study time doing things that are only indirectly associated with studying, not studying. Weak students often use the excuse of looking for things they need to do homework as procrastination to avoid that study and homework. This distraction simply prolongs the anticipated agony of real work and study.

Most items commonly used with study and homework should be located in designated areas - in the designated study area. Some of the most common items are:

Pencils	Pens	Notebook paper
Pencil sharpener	Compass	Protractor
Hole punch	Stapler	Paper clips
File folders	Rubber bands	Hi-lite markers
Dictionary	Thesaurus	Waste basket
Erasers	Alarm clock	Large calendar
Atlas	Ruler	Calculator

Why an alarm clock in the study area? The clock should be set for the planned study time, which will be discussed later. This allows focus on studying, not checking to see how much longer to study.

Fun books, books children enjoy reading, should be in the study area. When studying becomes tiring or tedious, the child can read a fun book to regain reading concentration. Reading without concentration serves no purpose.

A comfortable desk, table, or other flat surface should also be available to write on. A student who writes on a bed, sofa, or in his or her lap often develops sloppy penmanship. This often causes a student to earn bad grades, especially if the teacher can't read that writing.

Although this is a long list, most of these items are already available in most homes. Many of them, however, are moved from place to place and often are hard to find.

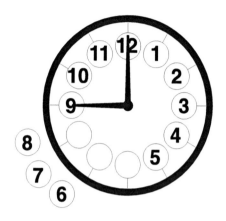

3

Set a routine study time

How often do children arrive home from school and announce, "I don't have any homework today?" Or, how often do they say, "I finished my homework at school?" Even worse, how often do they forget to do their homework?

A daily study time, at home, should be set by parents and students, regardless of the amount of homework. This creates a proactive approach to learning. It also indicates an acceptance by students and parents that the student's learning should not be determined only by the effectiveness and performance of the teacher. The child must accept responsibility for learning with the parent as a partner and guide.

Parents and students mutually should set a standard time for study. If more time is needed to complete homework, naturally that time should prevail. If the student has no homework, then he or she should use that time progressively for review, research, or improving other important skills such as reading.

The set study time should not be interpreted by the child as punishment. Talking about that time should be avoided during situations of frustration and stress between the parent and child, especially if that frustration and stress are caused by low grades. The topic should be discussed when the atmosphere is harmonious and friendly, and the conversation is focused on goals, success, and the future.

Study should not be continuous throughout the planned study time. Concentrated study time should be approximately fifteen to twenty minutes with five to ten minute rest intervals. For example, a one-hour study period would result in approximately forty-five minutes of actual study time. This schedule prevents aimless reading and drowsiness, satisfies the child's curiosity of events, and results in more effective study.

Routine and regular study time should be only part of a student's scheduled activities, since a child lives for things other than studying. The child and the parent should make sure time is also scheduled for playing, regular family fun activities, recreational activities, character building, and sleeping. These things are also important to one's development.

4

The parent must participate

Parents should be involved in, and part of, their children's study time and study effort, especially while their children are young. Even if the parent can't help with the actual homework, or doesn't have time to solve complicated math problems, the parent must show positive interest in the study process by asking questions and offering encouragement.

Two ideas are critical to help young children learn to read and enjoy learning to read. First, parents should ask about stories read or introduced in class each day. The child should have an opportunity to show he or she can remember those stories about Dick, Jane, and Spot, or whoever happens to be popular at the time.

Secondly, the parent should listen to the young child read to allow the child to feel important. A child must feel important to develop the necessary self-esteem to succeed.

Of course the approach will be different for older students, for they have different priorities. Although a parent wouldn't ordinarily listen to an older student read, the parent must still provide the interest, encouragement and opportunity for the child's self-esteem.

Research and surveys show that students from homes that have a culture of family participation in the study process are ordinarily more successful. They make better grades, they are happier people, and they tend to be more successful after graduation from school. Some research concludes that a child's grades are more often affected by the level of parental involvement in the study process than by the level of competency of the teacher or the education system.

5

Get enough exercise

Students often fail, or fail to do their best, because they ignore physical demands and physical capacities. Student health plays a major role in student success. It's often ignored, which causes conditions that might be interpreted as lack of motivation, lack of concern, or lack of ability.

Physical exercise is considered the most important health deficiency of students. Studies indicate the brain works at higher efficiency if it has a good blood supply with plenty of oxygen. A person who doesn't exercise sufficiently deprives his or her brain, and body, of at least some needed oxygen. Authorities suggest as many as forty percent of men students and seventy percent of women students fail to get enough exercise to provide the desired oxygen flow.

Students who appear lazy might not really be lazy; they might be doing the best they can. The best they can do, however, might be limited by the physical and mental deprivation they cause themselves by being too inactive or sedentary. They might be doing their best at that time, but that might not be the best they could do if they were active and healthy.

A student should schedule a time to exercise, with the same emphasis that he or she schedules a time to study. It's not essential it be hard and strenuous. It's not even necessary exercise be scheduled as exercise. Walking briskly is sufficient exercise if it's done routinely. The student may simply accomplish chores and errands by walking instead of riding to a different location to accomplish those tasks.

Younger students, in this age of computer games, often play those games for hours instead of playing in the traditional way that creates natural exercise. This includes running, jumping, climbing, and riding bicycles. Parents should insure their young children don't ignore these normal physical activities that will help keep them healthy. Children should be taught that a well-rounded schedule is healthier than an addiction to one activity.

6

Get enough sleep

Sleep is another important part of studying often overlooked or ignored. It's generally accepted that the average person, especially a younger person, needs at least eight hours sleep each night. Many need more than that, depending upon the person's individual personality and metabolism.

A young person, especially a student, expends much energy during a normal day. Although many students don't get enough physical exercise they still, nevertheless, expend energy. Young children play, which uses energy. Students must read, think, study, and perform in a classroom which also uses energy. Energy may be expended either mentally or physically. Energy is replenished during sleep, assuming of course the person does those other things necessary for health, such as eating the right food in the right amounts.

Sleep also allows other necessary things to happen to a person's body. It allows the body to eliminate toxins that accumulate during the day's activities. It also allows the body to repair itself in those areas where muscle and other tissues are strained or damaged. In summary, the body and the brain are allowed to rest and repair themselves.

The time for sleep must also be considered for sleep to have its best effect. Sleep is more effective if it's done at the same time - and in the same way. If a child is accustomed to going to bed at a certain time, then that time should be maintained as a regular schedule. One's body adjusts to a standard routine. If that routine changes, it takes the body some time to adjust to the new routine. If a person goes to bed at different times, his or her body might never become adjusted, calm, and comfortable. This is the body condition often referred to as 'jet lag.'

Older students should schedule their time for sleep with the same emphasis they schedule their time for study and for recreation. It's part of the over-all schedule, and just as important as any other study skill. Parents of younger children should insure their children develop a good sleep routine.

7

Don't be guided by peer pressure

Peer pressure is an influence that often discourages an otherwise good student from being a good student. Many students who have good intentions to study often are discouraged by pressure from their peers. Ordinarily, it's easy for most students to be influenced by their friends. They like their friends, they like to be around their friends, and they're comfortable with their friends. Unfortunately, negative peer pressure as well as positive peer pressure comes from one's friends. Only friends can use peer pressure. Who could be pressured by someone they didn't like into doing something they didn't want to do? Acquaintances who are disliked have no influence over a person.

How and why is peer pressure so powerful that it often replaces logic? Why is it so powerful that a person will often do something he or she knows is not the right thing to do? Peer pressure is powerful because it acts to fill basic needs that influence people.

According to motivation theories, people like to feel safe; they like to feel they belong to something important; and they like to feel respected. These likes are really needs. They need to feel safe. They need to feel they belong to something important. They need to feel respected, which creates a feeling of esteem.

Some peer pressure is positive, especially if the student is in a group with high ideals and high expectations of success. As a member of this group, a student tries to comply with the normal expectations (norms) of the group. These positive norms are respect for good grades, courtesy, understanding, and respect for each other's success.

A student who's part of a group with low ideals, low aspirations, and low self-esteem will most likely be influenced to comply with negative norms. In this negative group, a student who would mention success would be called a 'snob.' A student who attempts to make good grades would be branded a 'bookworm.' A student who tries to be respectful and courteous would be labeled a 'sissy.' A low-esteem group conditions and forces otherwise successful students to be low-achieving students.

Students with high potential and high ideals often trap themselves in negative groups that offer nothing but pressure to fail. This entrapment happens subtly and slowly. There are no bells, signs, or signals that announce: "You are now entering the influences of a low-esteem and negative group."

To remain free from the influences of a negative reference group, or low-esteem peer group, a student must make a positive and conscious effort to understand how negative peer pressure attacks a rational person, and how to avoid it. A student who's not alert might be drawn into the pits of negative peer pressure by a good friend.

The best way to avoid negative peer pressure is to develop a positive success plan and remain focused. Focusing on that goal will overcome most obstacles and distractions.

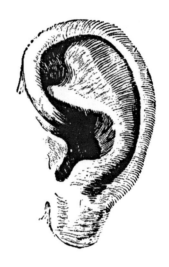

8

Learn to listen

Effective listening is a learned skill. It doesn't just happen. This is especially true in an environment where new concepts and ideas are introduced, such as in a school environment. In this environment, each word and each phrase are important to meaning and understanding.

Is listening easy? Is there no work to listening? Do you just let it happen? It's not easy; and there's lots of work to it. Let's explore some of the major problems that cause effective listening to be difficult.

It's not unusual for someone to drift off into nice thoughts and experience daydreams. Often a person daydreams when he or she is 'listening' to someone. It would be rare if that person could listen with understanding if his or her thoughts were focused in another area. To listen with understanding - the purpose for listening - one must not only hear those spoken words, one must also actively identify and interpret each word or thought.

A person's opinion of the speaker often influences effective listening. One who listens to a friend, or to someone he or she likes, will be more open and receptive to those words and ideas. One who must listen to someone who's disliked, or someone who causes frustration, will often ignore the meaning of important words from that person. For example, it might be difficult for a student to concentrate on information given by a teacher he or she dislikes. That might cause those words to have less meaning and validity.

Another example is the relationship between the teacher and the parent. If the parent likes the teacher, the parent will be more inclined to listen to the teacher's suggestions for helping a child study. If a parent doesn't like or trust the teacher, the child's low grades will more likely be attributed to the bad teacher. The parent might regard a teacher's instructions as excuses and self-justifications.

Teacher's also have their biases. Perhaps they don't listen to a child or his or her parents because the child is regarded as an undesirable or a trouble-maker with bad parents who don't care. In many cases the child might suffer from an emotional disorder or an attention disorder, which makes positive listening difficult. Good communications must exist in all areas associated with a student for a student to gain the most from studying. The student must listen, with meaning, to learn. Parents and teachers must also really listen to help with that student's learning process.

9

Learn to take notes

Some students think they can remember what the teacher says in class. They feel they are intelligent and have good memories. Consequently, those students think it's a waste of time and effort to take notes. Students should know why it's important to take notes, how to take notes, and how to use those notes. Parents and teachers must be prepared to teach young students how to take and use notes.

Learning, especially for class work, is basically an exercise in remembering. A student must learn to remember basic facts and ideas before he or she can use those basics to form concepts and higher ideas. Remembering has a certain reinforcement schedule.

Ordinarily, something initially learned is forgotten in the first eight hours. It's forgotten, unless it has reinforcement. After only one positive reinforcement event, that fact or idea might not be forgotten for thirty days or longer. Another reinforcement event might make the memory last for several months. Of course the point is reached where additional reinforcement adds no significant value to memory.

Notes make reinforcement of memory easy and convenient. If a student takes notes during a lecture or discussion, that student doesn't have to try to remember and recall the complete lecture. If a student doesn't take notes, and the same information is not in a book, chances are the student will not remember any part of the lecture the next day unless the teacher reviews that lecture. The student must take notes, for the teacher might not repeat and review that same information.

Note-taking in class should be simple enough to allow the student to listen to the teacher while writing notes. If the student is concentrating on taking such thorough notes that he or she doesn't understand the lesson, the student might miss other important concepts and information. Notes taken during a lecture should be words or phrases that identify important information.

The student must organize his or her notes as soon as possible, preferably within a few hours. Remember, after eight hours most memory is lost if it's not reinforced. While the student is expanding those notes, he or she should also recall other information the teacher emphasized and add that to the notes. Revised notes should be complete, but they should also be condensed. A student who tries to write too many notes will use valuable time that might be used better for another subject. Revised notes should have space to add additional comments as they are remembered when the student reviews those notes.

In summary, the student should routinely review notes. The first review must be within a few hours, before the most important information is forgotten. The second review may be after a longer period. Further review depends upon how well the student remembers the material during his or her review. Once the material is learned there's no reason to over learn. That time might be needed to study another subject, or to organize notes from another class.

The student must not wait until the night before a test to review notes. The normal learning curve will not allow necessary memory reinforcement.

10

Learn to outline or hi-lite

Students often open a book, read its words, then close it without remembering what the first paragraph said. When they read the book later as a review or to study for a test, they don't review, they must read as though they had never read the material before, especially if they were daydreaming when they read it the first time.

A student who outlines or hi-lites reading material improves his or her learning skills and makes the review phase faster, easier and simpler. Two learning concepts help make these actions more effective studying.

First, if a student prepares an outline, that student is really organizing ideas. To organize ideas one must be alert and thinking. It's difficult to let one's mind daydream if that person is really active in the reading-organizing process. It gets the person actively involved in the message instead of merely letting his or her eyes see random words.

Secondly, a student who outlines adds reinforcement to the message. Reading the material is the first action, and writing the note is the second action which is reinforcement. It's easier to remember if an idea or a fact has reinforcement.

Outlining is more effective than hi-liting or underlining in a book, although hi-liting or underlining is better than neither. Hi-liting serves the same purposes as outlining. It occupies the reader's mind and provides reinforcement, for a student will usually give some second thought to decide what to hi-lite or underline.

Outlining and hi-liting offer another great advantage. If a student becomes skilled at outlining or hi-liting, the review process becomes quicker and easier. The student doesn't have to keep reading the complete material to review and prepare for tests. He or she simply studies the condensed material, with an occasional overview of the full material to insure no important points were missed.

Although it's easier to underline and hi-lite in a book or other study material, a student must learn to outline from those study references. Some books are loaned and students aren't allowed to mark in them. In this case, outlining is the only practical answer to easy study. Outlining also allows the student to put related and similar information in the same group for better understanding.

11

Use flash cards

Using flash cards is a proven study skill, especially for younger students. Young children usually have shorter attention spans. They concentrate on something for a short time and then lose interest. Flash cards create the idea of a game, which is more fun than studying. They also fit into the short attention span of a young child. Each new flash card is a new subject to attract his or her interest.

For young children flash cards should be simple and convey only one bit of information. For example, flash cards for addition problems should have only one question and one answer on each card. Flash cards can be made on standard index cards or any other standard paper that's easy to handle. Parents should always help their young children with flash cards. Parents' involvement helps keep the child's interest focused on the importance of study time. It also helps to establish discipline in the study process. Flash cards may also be used effectively for older students. An older student would more likely consider them note cards instead of flash cards.

Older students should have note cards for important concepts and ideas a teacher might ask on a test. They should also have note cards for standard formulas and equations that must be memorized to solve mathematical problems. Anything that pertains to a definite concept or something that must be memorized should be on a note card.

Older students should have their important note cards with them at all times. It doesn't matter if they get bent and crinkled in one's pocket. The service they provide is more important than how they look. They should be used anytime a student is waiting for something to happen or looking for something to do. Students will be surprised how much time they spend just waiting. They should use their flash/note cards during these waiting periods,

12

Improve reading skills

A student often misses key ideas and facts while studying, not because the student isn't smart, but because the student doesn't understand how to read effectively. Usually, a student who reads words slowly and carefully is concentrating on words and not thoughts and ideas those words create. Thoughts must be understood to make sense from reading. One who doesn't know how to identify those thought signals cannot make the best use of study time.

Books and other reading material have signals that tell the reader which words and thoughts are important and which are support material, definition material, or explanation material. Some signals are determined by their location in the writing and some are determined by preparatory words.

Most study and homework are from textbooks. Most textbooks are written in the common format of chapters, paragraphs, and sentences. If a student understands how these segments are arranged, he or she may learn to pick out the key points from other support information.

Book chapters are divided into paragraphs. Ordinarily, the first paragraph in each chapter tells what the chapter is about. This gives a clue to the important points in the chapter. The last paragraph often summarizes the important information in the chapter. It should reinforce the first paragraph. Before reading a chapter, the student should read and understand the first and last paragraphs. That understanding will make the chapter have more meaning.

Paragraphs usually have signals that alert readers to the main points. These are in the form of topic sentences. Topic sentences are usually first in the paragraph, but not necessarily. Often, the first sentence is an introduction to the topic sentence. Topic sentences are easy to recognize after only a little practice. A student must know they exist, however, to learn how to recognize them.

Individual sentences also have signals that say, 'Okay, here comes an important point - pay attention.' These signals are special words such as: now, therefore, however, except, greatest, important event, at this time, currently, solution, idea and theory. Many others exist and may be identified merely by looking for them.

Students often have an assignment to read only part of a chapter. When this happens the student should also read the first and last paragraphs. It reminds the student what the chapter is about, and the purpose for that reading.

A student should never read assigned homework without having a dictionary within easy reach. Children will often skip over a word they don't understand, and it might be the most important word in the reading assignment. If it's an unusual word it will most likely be a word used in a test. A student should automatically learn the definition to any word that he or she doesn't understand. If a dictionary isn't nearby, that word might remain a mystery to the student.

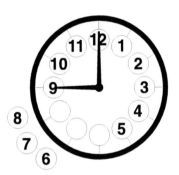

13

Use a timer while studying

If a student plans to study for an hour, he or she shouldn't spend much of that hour watching a clock to see how much longer to study. A student's mind must be focused on a subject to get the most from study time.

Five minutes of focused and concentrated study is better than an hour of studying while wondering about the time. It's difficult to interpret ideas, meanings, and concepts while reading if one wonders how much longer to study. Ordinarily, if the interest is split while reading, the reader sees only words, not ideas. The purpose for study is to remember important ideas. A timer allows one to concentrate on his or her studies.

14

Create a good environment

The quality of a student's home environment directly affects the ability, the interest, and the motivation for a student to study and to learn. Everyone in the home is responsible for the quality of life in that home to create those conditions that allow effective study.

The student must consider himself or herself a vital part of the family. As such, the student is as responsible for conditions in the home environment as any other member of the family. Those conditions must be supportive and harmonious to allow and encourage positive actions by all members of the family; not a negative environment that creates discouragement and despair.

Parents must be the leaders in the home to set the example of a comfortable home environment. In many cases the example the parent sets is the only condition children understand. If a parent is autocratic, domineering, and unreasonable, the child will assume that's normal for a family environment. That is until the child visits families of friends who live in homes with more love and understanding.

A home environment that's ruled by loud voices, defensive justifications, threats, violence, and the unending effort to prove oneself 'right' will be focused on personality and meaningless trivia rather than on progress and meaningful goals. A child's personality and interests will be handicapped in such a negative environment.

Parents must be aware of this handicap they place on their children if they don't maintain an atmosphere in the home that will allow the student to focus on study, grades, and meaningful success. It's not unusual for the parent who screams loudest at their children for making bad grades to be the source of those bad grades by the ringing of those screams in the child's head. It's not unusual for the parent who condemns teachers most harshly for causing their children not to learn properly to prevent that learning by their harshness that distracts from that positive learning. It's just as common for some parents to blame their children for lack of interest and concern about grades when those parents never offer to help their children with homework or to prepare for a test.

A young student will have no defenses against the ravages of an unhealthy home environment. Some young students may be successful because they like their teachers, because that's simply their natural personality, or because they have good friends who make good grades.

Older students have options once they know the home environment might contribute to their inability to focus on real and positive learning. They may try to explain the problem in the family; which might not have positive effects, for a defensive and autocratic parent would not accept the possibility that he or she could be the cause. They may find a location outside the home to study, at a routine time. The best solution, if possible, is to become part of a study group that's concerned about grades and personal success.

Teachers ordinarily recognize students who are performing at less than their reasonable ability; but the cause of that deficiency is often attributed to low motivation. Low motivation always has a cause. A negative home environment is one of those major causes. A teacher who recognizes or suspects a negative home environment as the source of a student's despair and low grades should encourage that student to find a friendly study location, perhaps the library, or to join a friendly and progressive study group.

Students and parents aren't the only people in homes who cause or create negative environments. Siblings often create that conflict and turmoil. It's the parents' duty to control those siblings to allow a child time to study without interference.

15

Choose successful friends

One's friends often determine the attitude that person will develop. Although another study skill cautioned about the influence of negative peer pressure, there's another influence that develops without pressure. That involves self-image and self-expectations. A person who thinks well of himself or herself, one who has real self-esteem, will become comfortable with other people who share those same traits.

There's an old saying, 'Birds of a feather flock together.' In applying this saying to people suggests those who regard themselves as successful, worthy, positive, and self-aware prefer to be with other people who share those same qualities. In school, these are ordinarily the students who respect themselves and other people, they have their homework prepared, they cooperate with teachers and administrators, and they participate in positive group activities.

There ordinarily are two other identifiable groups in schools. Those who flock together with negative attitudes and low self-esteem, and those who isolate themselves to remain alone, probably also from low self-esteem and insecurity. The student who remains alone may be driven to good grades to compensate for that loneliness and that feeling of insecurity. Even with good grades, however, that person remains handicapped in the success process, for a person ordinarily must know how to interact with other people to be successful.

The group that flocks together from common negative characteristics reinforces negative expectations within the group, even without peer pressure. Within that social cluster, low performance, low expectations, and low aspirations are the norms. Being successful is considered an alien condition that exists in other groups.

The positive group will say:

"When are we going to do that?"
"Do you want the homework typed or handwritten?"
"Let's get together after school and study math."
"What club or school activity do you belong to?"

The negative group will say:

"Do we really have to do that?"
"Do we have to turn in homework?"
"Let's leave school early today, or just skip."
"I stay away from all those clubs."

A positive student should become part of that positive group or, at minimum, feel that he or she is part of the positive group. This creates a feeling of normal success that makes study seem more natural.

16

Set realistic goals

Study goals should be reasonable and realistic. A student who routinely makes D and C grades shouldn't plan to make all A grades on the next report card. Although that might be possible, if the student had been a real slacker, it's not a practical approach. The student should plan to make some improvement, but not necessarily to take a giant step. The parent must be just as patient.

A student must change many things to improve his or her grades. All those things cannot be changed immediately. Study time must increase, without causing the student to become tired and weary. This includes a learning and adaptation process. Adjusting to a new study location takes time. Changing one's attitude about himself or herself takes time. One doesn't immediately change a negative self-image into a positive self-image without many 'little wins' along the way to keep that positive self-image growing. Long trips are taken with single small steps. Learning to improve grades requires that same approach. The good part, however, is that any improvement is positive improvement and reinforces the learning process.

One grade reporting cycle might not be enough to create any visible grade improvement for a student who starts with no disciplined study skills. At that time much of the focus of the student will be on the system and the method, not necessarily on effective study. There's also the possibility the next grade reporting cycle or test cycle might cover material that's unusually difficult.

Although earning good grades is important, in the beginning a student must focus more on the discipline of study than on the results of study. The student can control the discipline of study but not necessarily the results. Results will eventually occur when the student learns the process and the discipline. Ordinarily, the only difference between a C grade and a B grade is simply a little more effective study time.

Students and parents must also remember that grades may improve without that improvement being visible on a report card. For example, a grade of C might be earned with a grade average of 70 through 80. A student who improves his or her average from 70 to 80 makes a significant improvement. That should be considered one of the 'little wins' to add reinforcement and encouragement to keep improving.

Goals must be set high enough to offer a challenge and encouragement. They shouldn't be set so high they create defeat and lost aspirations. They often create worse despair if they can't be achieved.

17

Trust yourself and like yourself

Self-confidence, self-esteem, and success are things that grow together to become mutually supportive. A person who's successful will have self-confidence and self-esteem. A person who's confident will usually be successful and be proud of that success. A person who values personal pride and esteem will ordinarily be successful and confident. Since these traits accompany each other, a student may begin a good study skills program by focusing on either trait.

When first beginning to learn good study skills positive results might not begin immediately. It might take some time to learn those skills. Learning study skills is similar to learning anything else. One doesn't become a skilled ice-skater with just one lesson. That takes years. One doesn't become a professional basketball player by knowing how to bounce a basketball. That takes years of practice. One doesn't become an effective public speaker by being able to talk. That also takes knowledge and practice, including a combination of acceptable personality traits.

People become proficient in something in large part because they like themselves and they trust themselves and their dedication. A person who wants to become a professional ice-skater doesn't become discouraged and quit with the first fall, or the second, or the third. That person falls hundreds of times but never gives up. A basketball player doesn't quit when he or she misses a shot, or a thousand shots. The self-confidence keeps that person practicing one more time. A public speaker doesn't quit the first time he or she forgets a quote or becomes embarrassed before a crowd. That speaker does it one more time until it becomes natural. These winners have two special traits. They like themselves and they trust themselves.

Becoming a good student, learning good study skills, requires the same traits and dedication as becoming effective in any other facet of life. A student who likes himself or herself and who trusts himself or herself will not become discouraged and quit trying after the first fall or the first miss. That student will have the courage and dedication to try one more time.

In his book, *The Power of Positive Thinking*, Norman Vincent Peale advises, "When tackling a problem the number one thing is, never quit attacking it." Robert Schuller advises in his book, *Possibility Thinking*, "Great people are just ordinary people with an extraordinary amount of determination."

18

Don't be afraid to ask for help

Many people, including students, are afraid to ask a question or to ask for help. They don't like to ask questions for different reasons, which include:

1. They are too shy to ask.
2. They don't know how to ask the question.
3. They don't like the person they must ask.
4. They think it will make them look stupid.
5. They think the other person dislikes them.

6. They think the question isn't important.

Asking questions serves two valuable purposes. First is the obvious purpose; it creates answers to questions. If a question exists, then it's important to someone to have the answer. This is particularly valuable for a student, for one question might provide the clue to many answers.

Secondly, asking questions forces a person to interact with other people; which is itself a valuable experience. In his book, *Our Troubled Selves*, Allan Fromme writes, "Alone, we think less of ourselves, for sooner or later we feel rejected." He states further, "Separation from people usually becomes painful."

A student should try to find answers and solve problems by himself or herself; but that effort shouldn't become so laborious that it turns to frustration and despair. That feeling defeats the learning approach.

If possible, the student should ask the question to the teacher who teaches the subject that has the difficult question. Often, however, the student might not be comfortable talking with that teacher. In that case the student should discuss the question with another teacher, or with a student who most probably knows the answer. Most people like to be asked questions, if it's on a subject they understand. Recognizing their knowledge and ability is a compliment to them.

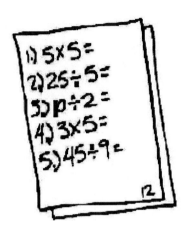

19

Learn how to take tests

A student should understand what tests are and how to take them before he or she begins to take tests. One should become test-wise in the art of testmanship. If not, that student is not prepared to do his or her best. Only a brief summary of testmanship skills will be identified here. Books are available in bookstores and libraries that give more in-depth details. Key points to taking tests include:

Review test material before the test. If the student has developed good study skills, most information will already have been learned. A review before the test, however, is necessary to test the

70

student's memory and to reinforce important specific facts. Pay close attention to topic sentences in the basic reading material, and compare those to notes, outlines, and flash cards.

Get enough rest and sleep the night before the test. A tired mind and body are less likely to allow information to be recalled. Some tests, themselves, are physically and mentally tiring.

Understand the instructions. In the lower grades these instructions will normally be given orally by the teacher. In the higher grades, the instructions are often written at the beginning of the test. In either case, those instructions must be understood to insure questions are answered in the right manner and order, and not in reverse. Understanding the testing process is as important as knowing the answers.

Know how much time is allowed for the test. Scan through the test material to see how much time may be allowed for each section, or part. Will more time be needed for essay questions, or does the test require only choice answers?

Stay alert to key words in the test. For example, true-false tests often give clues to answers by words such as always, never, all and none. If you must guess for a true-false answer, the answer should be your strongest first impression, or 'false.'

Answer the easy questions first. This serves two purposes. First, the student knows how much time he or she has left to consider the difficult questions. Easy questions will not be left unanswered if there's not enough time to complete the test. Secondly, answering the easy questions first often provides information or clues to answer the more difficult questions. Work on the more difficult questions next. Don't use too much time thinking about the same question, unless it's the last question.

Understand the different types of tests. These include:

* **True-false**
* **Multiple choice**
* **Matching**
* **Fill in the blanks**
* **Essay**

Each type of test has its special character that must be learned. As stated above, true-false tests have exclusionary words that suggest a false answer. Multiple choice questions usually have two answers that are clearly wrong. Matching questions usually have the same number of questions as answers. If one doesn't fit at the end, then one or more of the answered questions must be wrong. A fill in the blank question might give clues from other questions. Essay questions usually ask the student to inform, describe, explain or justify. The student must know the different meanings of these words. Books are available in libraries and bookstores that explain these different tests in more detail.

20

Reward yourself

Good things should be reinforced to make them happen again. This is a process called *positive reinforcement*. Although positive reinforcement is normally used incorrectly and abused, it should be used to enhance learning skills.

Positive reinforcement often is attempted by parents who promise to pay their children money for making good grades. This system seldom works because the money is a promise and becomes an indebtedness if the child improves his or her grades. It's not a reinforcing reward. For effective reinforcement the reward should be given by the parent, or teacher, after the good performance, without specifically applying that reward to that performance. The child must be allowed to make that association by himself or herself. That association of action and results, not the promise of a reward, creates the reinforcement.

On the other hand, the child should openly celebrate and reward himself or herself for hard work and sincere efforts. If the student is an older child, perhaps he or she should treat himself or herself to a special movie, a party, or an extra large banana split. For the younger child, perhaps a trip to the zoo or a nearby fishing hole would be appropriate.

In any event, the reward should be based on hard work, effort, and sincerity, not necessarily grades. Good grades are only the result of that effort. If a child works hard to learn good study skills and doesn't make better grades on the next test, that effort should still be rewarded. Good grades will eventually occur if the student doesn't become handicapped by disappointment and despair.

SUMMARIZED STUDY SKILLS
FOR
BEGINNING STUDENTS

1. HAVE A PLACE TO STUDY: You must have a good place to study. It should be a place where you go to study each time. It should also be a place that's quiet but not so quiet you feel isolated from everyone else. Your study area should be well lighted so you can read better, and should be well ventilated to prevent being sleepy.

2. GET YOUR STUDY THINGS TOGETHER: Everything you need to study and do your homework should be in your study area. This keeps you from wasting time looking for those things such as; pencils, pens, paper, pencil sharpener, atlas, stapler ruler, markers, compass, protractor and dictionary.

3. HAVE A SET STUDY TIME: Even if you don't have homework, you should have a set time to study every day. If possible, you should also study extra even when you have homework. This keeps you from falling behind, and lets you learn difficult things faster - especially good reading.

4. ASK YOUR PARENTS TO HELP: You should try to get your parents to help you study. If they help you they can explain some things faster than you can learn them by yourself. Any relative or older friend can also help you study.

5. BE HEALTHY - GET ENOUGH EXERCISE: It's very important for you to get enough exercise. Many students are unhealthy, or they get tired easily because they don't exercise enough to have energy and stamina to study enough.

6. BE HEALTHY - GET ENOUGH SLEEP: You can't think and learn very well if you are tired and sleepy. To do your best in school you must get enough sleep. Most people need at least eight hours of sleep to do their best.

7. AVOID PEER PRESSURE: Sometimes your friends will want you to do things you know you shouldn't do. For example, they might want you to play basketball or football at the same time you know you should be doing your homework. This is called 'peer pressure.'

8. LEARN TO REALLY LISTEN: To learn in class you must first learn how to really listen. Sometimes students think they are listening to the teacher, but they really are not. They might be hearing the teacher's words but their thoughts might be lost in a daydream.

9. LEARN HOW TO REMEMBER: Some students think they can't learn well because they don't know how to make good grades. Learning is just remembering important information. To help you remember, you should make notes while listening to your teacher. If you make notes, you can let your mind rest for awhile, while the information is kept on a piece of paper.

10. LEARN TO OUTLINE: You should learn to outline or hi-lite what you read. First, it will help you think about what you are reading without your mind wandering off. It also helps you learn to recognize the important ideas to remember.

11. USE FLASH CARDS: Another good way to learn and study for tests is to use flash cards. Your flash cards can be used for quick study time, and to reinforce memory of important information.

12.USE A TIMER TO STUDY: Use a timer, such as an alarm clock, when you study. This helps you think about studying and not about how much time you have left to study.

13. HELP CREATE A FRIENDLY FAMILY: Studying and learning are easier for you if you are part of a friendly, caring, and loving family. A family in which each person doesn't respect each other's feelings will think about more negative things than positive things. To learn better, you must think about positive things.

14. ASK FOR HELP: Learn to ask for help when you need help. Many people don't learn as much because they are afraid to ask. Sometimes they are too shy, or they think their question is not important. If you need to know something, go ahead and ask.

15. LEARN TO READ BETTER: You must know how to read well to learn something faster and easier. Some people think they are not smart, when they are really smarter than they think. They just haven't practiced reading enough to read faster and with more understanding. **Practice - practice - practic**e, all you can.

About The Author

Will Clark's author experiences began by writing inspection and evaluation reports in the U.S. Air Force. He is a retired Air Force officer and a Vietnam veteran, serving in Saigon from 1966 to 1967. His other overseas assignments include Misawa, Japan and Ankara, Turkey. He taught on-base college courses while stationed in Ankara.

In 1995, as a 'Friends of Education' study skills project, he authored a book, *How to Learn*, to encourage students to improve their grades in DeSoto County, Mississippi. Education supporters printed and distributed four thousand copies. He also wrote a weekly education column for a local newspaper, *The Desoto County Tribune*, the following school year. He also taught an adult GED class. His book, *How to Learn*, has been updated and is now available everywhere.

His next published book was *School Bells and Broken Tales*, a parody of nursery rhyme characters, also a motivation and education book for children. His other books include *Shades of Retribution*, a historical novel, and *Simply Success*, a motivation guide for students and employees.

His latest action novel, *The Atlantis Crystal*, is the first of a trilogy based on Atlantis and crystals. The other two, coming soon, are: *She Waits in Atlantis*, and *The Burning Crystal*. This trilogy is based on his travels while assigned to Turkey, site of the ancient city of Troy.

He is a past member of Toastmasters, a life member of Optimists International, a past Optimist Club president and a past Optimist area lieutenant governor.

Study

Learn

Succeed

Have Fun

Other Books by Will Clark

Novels
The Atlantis Crystal
Shades of Retribution

Juvenile - Children
Wishing Wells and Broken Tales
Forest Trails and Fairy Tales

Non-Fiction
How To Learn
The Peer Pressure Monster
Speak Without Fear
The Education Jungle
Simply Success

Notes

Notes

Notes

Notes

Notes

Notes

Notes

Notes

Notes

Notes

Notes

Notes

Notes

Notes

Notes

Notes

Notes

Notes

Notes

LaVergne, TN USA
30 March 2011
222221LV00004B/5/P